Ancient Moorish Literature

Charles F. Horne

Kessinger Publishing's Rare Reprints

Thousands of Scarce and Hard-to-Find Books on These and other Subjects!

- Americana
- Ancient Mysteries
- Animals
- Anthropology
- Architecture
- Arts
- Astrology
- Bibliographies
- Biographies & Memoirs
- Body, Mind & Spirit
- Business & Investing
- Children & Young Adult
- Collectibles
- Comparative Religions
- Crafts & Hobbies
- Earth Sciences
- Education
- Ephemera
- Fiction
- Folklore
- Geography
- Health & Diet
- History
- Hobbies & Leisure
- Humor
- Illustrated Books
- Language & Culture
- Law
- Life Sciences
- Literature
- Medicine & Pharmacy
- Metaphysical
- Music
- Mystery & Crime
- Mythology
- Natural History
- Outdoor & Nature
- Philosophy
- Poetry
- Political Science
- Science
- Psychiatry & Psychology
- Reference
- Religion & Spiritualism
- Rhetoric
- Sacred Books
- Science Fiction
- Science & Technology
- Self-Help
- Social Sciences
- Symbolism
- Theatre & Drama
- Theology
- Travel & Explorations
- War & Military
- Women
- Yoga
- *Plus Much More!*

We kindly invite you to view our catalog list at:
http://www.kessinger.net

MOORISH LITERATURE

SCIENCE AND HISTORY AMONG
THE MOORS

"*The religion sacred to philosophers is to study that which* IS, *for the most sublime worship one can render to God is the recognition and knowledge of his works.*"
                                              —AVERROES.

MOORISH LITERATURE

SCIENCE AND HISTORY

(INTRODUCTION)

THE name "Moor" is used loosely to describe all those peoples who sprang from the mingling of the Berber, or Hamitic, stock of North Africa, with the Arabs or Semitic stock who swept over the region in the Mohammedan conquest. The chief achievement of this mixed or Moorish race was the establishment of their brilliant kingdom and independent caliphate in Spain. Under the most powerful of these Spanish caliphs, Ahderrahman III. (A.D. 912–961), their capital Cordova had six hundred mosques, including its still celebrated chief mosque, the most beautiful building of that age in Europe. The Moorish kingdom of Spain had then seventeen universities and over seventy large libraries. It was the most cultured land of Europe, the goal of scholars from less peaceful and less learned Christendom.

The Moorish kingdom in the course of the twelfth century broke up into many tiny States. These soon fought among themselves and plunged each other into a common ruin. African Moors, of far more ignorant and fanatic type, came to aid their Spanish brethren; and under the pressure of these barbarians, culture rapidly declined. The universities were broken up. The great scholar Averroes, who had been the pride of his nation, was accused of heresy. His teachings were found not sufficiently subservient to the Koran; and finally, in 1195, he was driven into exile. This event, or Averroes' death soon afterward, may be reckoned as marking the downfall of the Moorish leadership in science and philosophy.

In our volume we give some of Averroes' most celebrated

237

commentaries, as typifying the culmination of Moorish culture.   We give also, as its opening note, the speech with which Tarik, the first conqueror of Spain, in the year A.D. 711 led his army to cross the Straits of Gibraltar and began the attack upon the earlier Christian inhabitants.   This speech does not, however, preserve the actual words of Tarik; it only presents the tradition of them as preserved by the Moorish historian Al Maggari, who wrote in Africa long after the last of the Moors had been driven out of Spain.   In Al Maggari's day the older Arabic traditions of exact service had quite faded.   The Moors had become poets and dreamers instead of scientists and critical historians.   The very name of Al Maggari's history may be accepted as typifying its character.   He called it "Breath of Perfumes."

SCIENCE AND HISTORY

PHILOSOPHIC THOUGHTS

(By Averroes)

The first to preach the resurrection were the prophets of
Israel after Moses, then the Evangelical Christians, then the
Sabians, whose religion has been called by Ibn-Hazm the old-
est in the world. The reason so many founders of religion
established this dogma was because they supposed this belief
would moralize men and induce them to be virtuous in their
own interests. I do not quarrel with Al Ghazali or Motecal-
lemin for saying that the soul is immortal, but I object to the
idea that the soul is a mere accident, and that a man can take
again the body which has fallen into decay. No, he may take
another, similar to the first, but that which has been dead can
not return to life. These two bodies are only one, viewed
as a species, but they are two in number. Aristotle has said
in the last lines of his " Generation and Corruption ": " A
body once corrupted can never become the same again; it
can never return as an individual whole, but it can return
to the specific variety of which it is a part. When air separates from water or water separates from air, each of these
substances can not become again the thing it was, but must
return to its own species."

How have we come to adopt these tales of the creation?
Through habit. Just as a man inured to poison can take it
with impunity, so a man used to them from childhood can
accept the most unbelievable opinions. Therefore the opinions of the masses are only formed through habit. The people believe that which they hear incessantly repeated. And
that is why the power of religion is so much stronger than
that of philosophy, for it is not accustomed to hearing the
opposite of its belief, a thing which happens very often to

philosophy: So one sees frequently, nowadays, men who, having entered suddenly into the study of the speculative sciences, lose the religious beliefs which they have only held through habit, and become *zendiks* (infidels).

The religion sacred to philosophers is to study that which *is,* for the most sublime worship one can render to God is the recognition and knowledge of his works, which leads us to know him, himself, in all his *reality.* In the eyes of God that is the noblest action, while the vilest action is to tax with error and presumption those who practise this worship, higher than any other, who adore him by this religion, the best of all religions.

Among the most dangerous of these fictions concerning a future life are those which counsel virtue as a means of arriving at happiness. In that case virtue is no longer worth anything, since one only abstains from voluptuousness in the hope of being doubly repaid in the future. The brave will only seek death to evade a worse evil. The good will only respect the belongings of others in order to acquire twice as much.

Wine is forbidden because it excites wickedness and quarrels; but I am preserved from those excesses by wisdom: I take it only to sharpen my wits.[1]

That renegade philosopher, Al Ghazali, has gathered up all he learned from the writings of the philosophers, and has turned against them the arms he borrowed from them.

As for us, the philosophers, at the risk of exposing ourselves to the rage of the persecutors of philosophy, which was

[1] It is unfortunate that both the philosopher and his opponents should have advanced the same argument in defense of themselves — namely, their own wisdom. The Arab philosophers were, amongst their kind, something like the *libertins* of the seventeenth century in France. "Often," says Al Ghazali, "I have seen one read the Koran, assist at religious ceremonies and prayers, and praise religion aloud. When I asked him, 'If you consider prophetism as false, why do you pray?' he responded, 'It is an exercise of the body, a custom of the country, a method of having your life saved.' Yet he did not cease from drinking wine, and delivering himself to all sorts of abominations and impieties."

our mother, we will, when the time is ripe, uncover the poison hidden in Al Ghazali's book.

Our social state does not bring out all the resources and possibilities there are in women; it would seem that they are only destined to bear and rear children, and this state of servitude has destroyed in them the capability for larger things. That is why one never sees, with us, a woman possessed of the moral virtues — their lives pass like those of flowers, and they are a burden upon their husbands. From this comes also the misery which devours our cities, for there are twice as many women there as men, but the former are not permitted to work for their own support.

My father aided in rescuing from prison Ibn Badja, who was accused of heresy. My father does not understand that his own son will one day be regarded as a far worse heretic.

God alone knows if I am one; but it is absolutely certain that it was only the intrigues of my enemies which led to my condemnation. I thought only of editing Aristotle and establishing accord between religion and philosophy.

TARIK'S ADDRESS TO HIS SOLDIERS

(FROM THE HISTORY OF AL MAGGARI)

When Tarik had been informed of the approach of the enemy, he rose in the midst of his companions and, after having glorified God in the highest, he spoke to his soldiers thus:

"Oh my warriors, whither would you flee? Behind you is the sea, before you, the enemy. You have left now only the hope of your courage and your constancy. Remember that in this country you are more unfortunate than the orphan seated at the table of the avaricious master. Your enemy is before you, protected by an innumerable army; he has men in abundance, but you, as your only aid, have your own swords, and, as your only chance for life, such chance as you can snatch from the hands of your enemy. If the absolute want to which you are reduced is prolonged ever so little, if you delay to seize immediate success, your good fortune will vanish, and your enemies, whom your very presence has filled with fear, will take courage. Put far from you the disgrace from which you flee in dreams, and attack this monarch who has left his strongly fortified city to meet you. Here is a splendid opportunity to defeat him, if you will consent to expose yourselves freely to death. Do not believe that I desire to incite you to face dangers which I shall refuse to share with you. In the attack I myself will be in the fore, where the chance of life is always least.

"Remember that if you suffer a few moments in patience, you will afterward enjoy supreme delight. Do not imagine that your fate can be separated from mine, and rest assured that if you fall, I shall perish with you, or avenge you. You have heard that in this country there are a large number of ravishingly beautiful Greek maidens, their graceful forms are draped in sumptuous gowns on which gleam pearls, coral, and purest gold, and they live in the palaces of royal kings. The Commander of True Believers, Alwalid, son of Abdalmelik, has chosen you for this attack from among all his Arab warriors; and he promises that you shall become his comrades and shall hold the rank of kings in this country. Such is his confidence in your intrepidity. The one fruit which he desires to obtain from your bravery is that the word of God shall be exalted in this country, and that the true religion shall be established here. The spoils will belong to yourselves.

"Remember that I place myself in the front of this glorious charge which I exhort you to make. At the moment when the two armies meet hand to hand, you will see me, never doubt it, seeking out this Roderick, tyrant of his people, challenging him to combat, if God is willing. If I perish after this, I will have had at least the satisfaction of delivering you, and you will easily find among you an experienced hero, to whom you can confidently give the task of directing you. But should I fall before I reach to Roderick, redouble your ardor, force yourselves to the attack and achieve the conquest of this country, in depriving him of life. With him dead, his soldiers will no longer defy you."

MOORISH LITERATURE

POETRY OF THE SPANISH MOORS

"*Fortune, that whilom owned my sway,*
And bowed obsequious to my nod,
Now sees me destined to obey,
And bend beneath oppression's rod."
— PRINCE MOHAMMED BEN ABAD.

POETRY OF THE SPANISH MOORS

(INTRODUCTION)

WHILE the scientific leadership of the Moors faded with
the breaking of their military unity in the twelfth century, they still retained in some of their smaller kingdoms,
and especially in that of Granada, a high degree of culture.
The love of beauty and the spirit of romance were strong
among all the Spanish Moors; and so their poetry continued
long after science failed them. Poetry indeed became their
main expression. Granada, the last of all their Spanish
kingdoms, did not fall before the advancing Christians until
1492. Then, as our histories have so often told, Ferdinand
and Isabella, the Christian rulers of Spain, conducted a
holy war for the destruction of Granada. Its last fortress
surrendered, and its people withdrew to Africa. There, ac-
cording to a characteristically dreamy legend, they still retain the keys of their mansions in Granada, treasuring them
up for the day of their triumphant return.

Of the Moorish poetry which survived the fall of Granada,
much was preserved by the Spaniards themselves and in the
Spanish language. The victors knew how to value the spirit
of the vanquished; and ballads of Moorish origin, telling of
Moorish loves, long remained popular in Spain. The au-
thors of most of these have been forgotten. The text of some
of the best known of them is given here.

MOORISH POETRY

VERSES TO MY DAUGHTERS [1]

(By Prince Mohammed ben Abad)

With jocund heart and cheerful brow
  I used to hail the festal morn —
How must Mohammed greet it now? —
  A prisoner helpless and forlorn.

While these dear maids in beauty's bloom,
  With want opprest, with rags o'erspread,
By sordid labors at the loom
  Must earn a poor, precarious bread.

Those feet that never touched the ground,
  Till musk or camphor strewed the way,
Now bare and swoll'n with many a wound,
  Must struggle through the miry clay.

Those radiant cheeks are veiled in woe,
  A shower descends from every eye,
And not a starting tear can flow,
  That wakes not an attending sigh.

Fortune, that whilom owned my sway,
  And bowed obsequious to my nod,

[1] Seville was one of those small sovereignties into which Spain had been divided after the extinction of the house of Ommiah. It did not long retain its independence, and the only prince who ever presided over it as a separate kingdom seems to have been Mohammed ben Abad, the author of these verses. For thirty-three years he reigned over Seville and the neighboring districts with considerable reputation, but being attacked by Joseph, son to the Emperor of Morocco, at the head of a numerous army of Africans, was defeated, taken prisoner, and thrown into a dungeon, where he died in the year A.D. 1087.

246

Now sees me destined to obey,
  And bend beneath oppression's rod.

Ye mortals with success elate,
  Who bask in hope's delusive beam,
Attentive view Mohammed's fate,
  And own that bliss is but a dream.

SERENADE TO MY SLEEPING MISTRESS [2]

(By Ali ben Abad)

Sure Harut's [3] potent spells were breathed
  Upon that magic sword, thine eye;
For if it wounds us thus while sheathed,
  When drawn, 'tis vain its edge to fly.

How canst thou doom me, cruel fair,
  Plunged in the hell [4] of scorn to groan?
No idol e'er this heart could share,
  This heart has worshiped thee alone.

THE INCONSISTENT [5]

When I sent you my melons, you cried out with scorn,
  They ought to be heavy and wrinkled and yellow;
When I offered myself, whom those graces adorn,
  You flouted, and called me an ugly old fellow.

[2] This author was by birth an African; but having passed over to Spain, he was much patronized by Mohammed, Sultan of Seville. After the fall of his master, Ben Abad returned to Africa, and died at Tangier, A.D. 1087.

[3] A wicked angel who is permitted to tempt mankind by teaching them magic; see the legend respecting him in the Koran.

[4] The poet here alludes to the punishments denounced in the Koran against those who worship a plurality of Gods: "Their couch shall be in hell, and over them shall be coverings of fire."

[5] Written to a lady upon her refusal of a present of melons, and her rejection of the addresses of an admirer.

THE BULL-FIGHT OF GAZUL [6]

King Almanzor of Granada, he hath bid the trumpet sound,
He hath summoned all the Moorish lords, from the hills and
    plains around;
From *vega* and *sierra,* from Betis and Xenil,
They have come with helm and cuirass of gold and twisted
    steel.

'Tis the holy Baptist's feast they hold in royalty and state,
And they have closed the spacious lists beside the Alhambra's
    gate;
In gowns of black and silver laced, within the tented ring,
Eight Moors to fight the bull are placed in presence of the
    King.

Eight Moorish lords of valor tried, with stalwart arm and
    true,
The onset of the beasts abide, as they come rushing through;
The deeds they've done, the spoils they've won, fill all with
    hope and trust,
Yet ere high in heaven appears the sun they all have bit the
    dust.

Then sounds the trumpet clearly, then clangs the loud tam-
    bour,
Make room, make room for Gazul — throw wide, throw wide
    the door;
Blow, blow the trumpet clearer still, more loudly strike the
    drum,
The *Alcaydé* of Algava to fight the bull doth come.

[6] Gazul is the name of one of the Moorish heroes who figure in the
"*Historia de las Guerras Civiles de Granada.*" The ballad is one of
very many in which the dexterity of the Moorish cavaliers in the bull-
fight is described. The reader will observe that the shape, activity,
and resolution of the unhappy animal destined to furnish the amuse-
ment of the spectators are enlarged upon, just as the qualities of a
modern race-horse might be among ourselves: nor is the bull without
his name. The day of the Baptist is a festival among the Mussulmans,
as well as among Christians.

And first before the King he passed, with reverence stooping
    low,
And next he bowed him to the Queen, and the *Infantas* all
    a-row;
Then to his lady's grace he turned, and she to him did throw
A scarf from out her balcony, 'twas whiter than the snow.

With the life-blood of the slaughtered lords all slippery is the
    sand,
Yet proudly in the center hath Gazul ta'en his stand;
And ladies look with heaving breast, and lords with anxious
    eye,
But firmly he extends his arm — his look is calm and high.

Three bulls against the knight are loosed, and two come roar-
    ing on,
He rises high in stirrup, forth stretching his *rejón;*
Each furious beast upon the breast he deals him such a blow
He blindly totters and gives back, across the sand to go.

" Turn, Gazul, turn! " the people cry — the third comes up
    behind,
Low to the sand his head holds he, his nostrils snuff the wind;
The mountaineers that lead the steers, without stand whisper-
    ing low,
" Now thinks this proud *alcaydé* to stun Harpado so ? "

From Guadiana comes he not, he comes not from Xenil,
From Gaudalarif of the plain, or Barves of the hill;
But where from out the forest burst Xarama's waters clear,
Beneath the oak-trees was he nursed, this proud and stately
    steer.

Dark is his hide on either side, but the blood within doth boil,
And the dun hide glows, as if on fire, as he paws to the tur-
    moil.
His eyes are jet, and they are set in crystal rings of snow;
But now they stare with one red glare of brass upon the foe.

Upon the forehead of the bull the horns stand close and near,
From out the broad and wrinkled skull, like daggers they appear;
His neck is massy, like the trunk of some old knotted tree,
Whereon the monster's shaggy mane, like billows curled, ye see.

His legs are short, his hams are thick, his hoofs are black as night,
Like a strong flail he holds his tail in fierceness of his might;
Like something molten out of iron, or hewn from forth the rock,
Harpado of Xarama stands, to bide the *alcaydé's* shock.

Now stops the drum — close, close they come — thrice meet, and thrice give back;
The white foam of Harpado lies on the charger's breast of black —
The white foam of the charger on Harpado's front of dun —
Once more advance upon his lance — once more, thou fearless one!

Once more, once more; — in dust and gore to ruin must thou reel —
In vain, in vain thou tearest the sand with furious heel —
In vain, in vain, thou noble beast, I see, I see thee stagger,
Now keen and cold thy neck must hold the stern *alcaydé's* dagger!

They have slipped a noose around his feet, six horses are brought in,
And away they drag Harpado with a loud and joyful din.
Now stoop thee, lady, from thy stand, and the ring of price bestow
Upon Gazul of Algava, that hath laid Harpado low.

THE ZEGRI'S BRIDE [7]

Of all the blood of Zegri, the chief is Lisaro,
To wield *rejón* like him is none, or javelin to throw;
From the place of his dominion, he ere the dawn doth go,
From Alcala de Henares, he rides in weed of woe.

He rides not now as he was wont, when ye have seen him speed
To the field of gay Toledo, to fling his lusty reed;
No gambeson of silk is on, nor rich embroidery
Of gold-wrought robe or turban — nor jeweled *tahali.*

No amethyst nor garnet is shining on his brow,
No crimson sleeve, which damsels weave at Tunis, decks him
    now;
The belt is black, the hilt is dim, but the sheathed blade is
    bright;
They have housened his barb in a murky garb, but yet her
    hoofs are light.

Four horsemen good, of the Zegri blood, with Lisaro go out;
No flashing spear may tell them near, but yet their shafts are
    stout;
In darkness and in swiftness rides every armed knight —
The foam on the rein ye may see it plain, but nothing else is
    white.

Young Lisaro, as on they go, his bonnet doffeth he,
Between its folds a sprig it holds of a dark and glossy tree;
That sprig of bay, were it away, right heavy heart had he —
Fair Zayda to her Zegri gave that token privily.

And ever as they rode, he looked upon his lady's boon.
"God knows," quoth he, "what fate may be — I may be
    slaughtered soon;

[7] The reader can not need to be reminded of the fatal effects which
were produced by the feuds subsisting between the two great families,
or rather races, of the Zegris and the Abencerrages of Granada. This
ballad is also from the "*Guerras Civiles.*"

Thou still art mine, though scarce the sign of hope that
    bloomed whilere,
But in my grave I yet shall have my Zayda's token dear."

Young Lisaro was musing so, when onward on the path,
He well could see them riding slow; then pricked he in his
    wrath.
The raging sire, the kinsmen of Zayda's hateful house,
Fought well that day, yet in the fray the Zegri won his
    spouse.

ZARA'S EARRINGS

" My earrings! my earrings! they've dropped into the well,
And what to say to Muça, I can not, can not tell."
'Twas thus, Granada's fountain by, spoke Albuharez' daugh-
    ter
" The well is deep, far down they lie, beneath the cold blue
    water —
To me did Muça give them, when he spake his sad farewell,
And what to say when he comes back, alas! I can not tell.

" My earrings! my earrings! they were pearls in silver set,
That when my Moor was far away, I ne'er should him forget,
That I ne'er to other tongue should list, nor smile on other's
    tale,
But remember he my lips had kissed, pure as those earrings
    pale —
When he comes back, and hears that I have dropped them in
    the well,
Oh, what will Muça think of me, I can not, can not tell.

" My earrings! my earrings! he'll say they should have been,
Not of pearl and of silver, but of gold and glittering sheen,
Of jasper and of onyx, and of diamond shining clear,
Changing to the changing light, with radiance insincere —

That changeful mind unchanging gems are not befitting
    well —
Thus will he think — and what to say, alas! I can not tell.

"He'll think when I to market went, I loitered by the way;
He'll think a willing ear I lent to all the lads might say;
He'll think some other lover's hand, among my tresses noosed,
From the ears where he had placed them, my rings of pearl
    unloosed;
He'll think, when I was sporting so beside this marble well,
My pearls fell in — and what to say, alas! I can not tell.

"He'll say, I am a woman, and we are all the same;
He'll say I loved when he was here to whisper of his flame —
But when he went to Tunis my virgin troth had broken,
And thought no more of Muça, and care not for his token.
My earrings! my earrings! O luckless, luckless well,
For what to say to Muça, alas! I can not tell.

"I'll tell the truth to Muça, and I hope he will believe —
That I thought of him at morning, and thought of him at eve;
That, musing on my lover, when down the sun was gone,
His earrings in my hand I held, by the fountain all alone;
And that my mind was o'er the sea, when from my hand they
    fell,
And that deep his love lies in my heart, as they lie in the
    well."

THE LAMENTATION FOR CELIN

At the gate of old Granada, when all its bolts are barred,
At twilight at the Vega gate there is a trampling heard;
There is a trampling heard, as of horses treading slow,
And a weeping voice of women, and a heavy sound of woe.
"What tower is fallen, what star is set, what chief come these
    bewailing?"
"A tower is fallen, a star is set.   Alas! alas for Celin!"

Three times they knock, three times they cry, and wide the
    doors they throw;
Dejectedly they enter, and mournfully they go;
In gloomy lines they mustering stand beneath the hollow
    porch,
Each horseman grasping in his hand a black and flaming
    torch;
Wet is each eye as they go by, and all around is wailing,
For all have heard the misery.   " Alas! alas for Celin! "—

Him yesterday a Moor did slay, of Bencerraje's blood,
'Twas at the solemn jousting, around the nobles stood;
The nobles of the land were by, and ladies bright and fair
Looked from their latticed windows, the haughty sight to
    share;
But now the nobles all lament, the ladies are bewailing,
For he was Granada's darling knight. " Alas! alas for
    Celin! "

Before him ride his vassals, in order two by two,
With ashes on their turbans spread, most pitiful to view;
Behind him his four sisters, each wrapped in sable veil,
Between the tambour's dismal strokes take up their doleful
    tale;
When stops the muffled drum, ye hear their brotherless be-
    wailing,
And all the people, far and near, cry —" Alas! alas for
    Celin! "

Oh! lovely lies he on the bier, above the purple pall,
The flower of all Granada's youth, the loveliest of them all;
His dark, dark eyes are closed, his rosy lip is pale,
The crust of blood lies black and dim upon his burnished
    mail,
And evermore the hoarse tambour breaks in upon their wail-
    ing,
Its sound is like no earthly sound —" Alas! alas for Celin! "

The Moorish maid at the lattice stands, the Moor stands at
    his door,
One maid is wringing of her hands, and one is weeping
    sore —
Down to the dust men bow their heads, and ashes black they
    strew
Upon their broidered garments of crimson, green, and blue —
Before each gate the bier stands still, then bursts the loud be-
    wailing,
From door and lattice, high and low —" Alas! alas for
    Celin! "

An old, old woman cometh forth, when she hears the people
    cry;
Her hair is white as silver, like horn her glazèd eye.
'Twas she that nursed him at her breast, that nursed him long
    ago;
She knows not whom they all lament, but soon she well shall
    know.
With one deep shriek she through doth break, when her ears
    receive their wailing —
" Let me kiss my Celin ere I die — Alas! alas for Celin! "

This is the end of this publication.

Any remaining blank pages are for our book binding
requirements and are blank on purpose.

To search thousands of interesting publications like this one,
please remember to visit our website at:

http://www.kessinger.net

www.ingramcontent.com/pod-product-compliance
Lightning Source LLC
LaVergne TN
LVHW080010070326
832903LV00069B/250